This journal belongs to:

____

I am loved and worthy of love.

Better Man

Month: _______________

Goal Type	Goals
Personal Goals	
Business Goals	
Self Care Goals	

How can I be the best version of myself this month?

____

____

____

____

Notes

I have unlimited potential and can achieve whatever I want to.

Better Man

Month: _______________

Goal Type	Goals
Personal Goals	
Business Goals	
Self Care Goals	

How can I be the best version of myself this month?

____

____

____

____

Notes

I am confident.

Better Man

Month: ________________

Goal Type	Goals
Personal Goals	
Business Goals	
Self Care Goals	

How can I be the best version of myself this month?

____

____

____

____

Notes

I am happy and excited about my life.

Better Man

Month: ______________

Goal Type	Goals
Personal Goals	
Business Goals	
Self Care Goals	

How can I be the best version of myself this month?

____

____

____

____

Notes

I let go of all my fears and trust that everything will turn out for the better.

Better Man

Month: _______________

Goal Type	Goals
Personal Goals	
Business Goals	
Self Care Goals	

How can I be the best version of myself this month?

____

____

____

____

Notes

Obstacles are moving out of my way.

Better Man

Month: _________________

Goal Type	Goals
Personal Goals	
Business Goals	
Self Care Goals	

How can I be the best version of myself this month?

____

____

____

____

Notes

My relationships
are becoming
stronger and
deeper with
each passing
day.

Better Man

Month: _______________

Goal Type	Goals
Personal Goals	
Business Goals	
Self Care Goals	

How can I be the best version of myself this month?

____

____

____

____

Notes

My life is full of prosperity and abundance.

Better Man

Month: _______________

Goal Type	Goals
Personal Goals	
Business Goals	
Self Care Goals	

How can I be the best version of myself this month?

____

____

____

____

Notes

People respect and value my opinions.

Better Man

Month: _______________

Goal Type	Goals
Personal Goals	
Business Goals	
Self Care Goals	

How can I be the best version of myself this month?

____

____

____

____

Notes

I am handsome.
I won't let
anyone tell me
otherwise.

Better Man

Month: ___________________

Goal Type	Goals
Personal Goals	
Business Goals	
Self Care Goals	

How can I be the best version of myself this month?

____

____

____

____

____

Notes

I am successful in all areas of my life.

Better Man

Month: ________________

Goal Type	Goals
Personal Goals	
Business Goals	
Self Care Goals	

How can I be the best version of myself this month?

____

____

____

____

____

Notes

I don't have to change myself to impress someone. I like who I am and I will never wear a mask to be someone that I am not.

Better Man

Month: ________________

Goal Type	Goals
Personal Goals	
Business Goals	
Self Care Goals	

How can I be the best version of myself this month?

____

____

____

____

Notes

Notes

Notes

Notes

Notes

Notes

Notes

Notes

Notes

Notes

Notes

Notes

Notes

Notes

Notes

Notes

Notes

Notes

Notes

Notes

Notes

Notes

Notes

Notes

Notes

Notes

Notes

Notes

Notes

Notes

Notes

Notes

Notes

Notes

Notes

Notes

Notes

Notes

Notes

Notes

Notes

Notes

Notes

Notes

Notes

Notes

Notes

Notes

Notes

Notes

Notes

Notes

Notes

Notes

Notes

Notes

Notes

Notes

Notes

Notes

Notes

Notes

Notes

Notes